Pensive 'Moods

A Book of Free Verse Poetry in Italian and English

Silence
Mile upon mile
Crisp winter air
CRACKLING ICE-WATER
Movement stealthy
Forms lapping ...WOLF PACK.
And silence broken
By baying of.....

A. Grebaz

To order additional copies of this book, contact:
Xlibris Corporation
1-888-795-4274
www.Xlibris.com
Orders@Xlibris.com
101256

Contents

Cibo 5

Food 6

Home 7

Nel Blu 9

In The Sky 10

Alpine Landscape 11

Seasons 13

Change 14

Needs 15

Tanka (Japanese Poetry) 17

Mystery Quest 18

Desert 19

Piccole Parole 20

Small Words 21

Take Time (To . . .) 22

Longing 23

Ma Qualche Volta I Sogni 24

But Sometime The Dreams 25

Tree 26

Fiery Phoenix 28

"Somewhere The Hurt . . ." 32

Spring 33

Storm 34

Wave 36

Le Tre Crime Del Lavaredo 37

The Three Peaks Of The Lavaredo 38

Sleeping Village 40

Una Rosa Tra Le Spine (Tina) 42

A Rose Among The Thorns (Tina) 43

Midnight Solitudes 45

Solitudini Notturne 46

Faces 47

Face 48

Life...49
Vita..50
Life's Meaning 52
The Ball 54
Where Eagles Fly 55
La Scogliera Dei Sogni Perduti.....................................56
The Cliff Of Lost Dreams 57
Storms 58
Foresta Boreale 59
Canadian Shield 61
Quench, Oh Pen 64
Sazia, O Penna 65
You 70
Once Upon A Seashore 71
Each Day 72
Ogni Giorno 73
Creativity...75
Sliver Of A Moon 76
A Walk In Time 78
Harbingers Of Spring 80
A Heart Of Stone 81
Mare 83
Sea 84
Someday 85
Forse Un Giorno 86
Words, Like A Fountain, Flow 88
Silenzio..89
Silence...91
Heart..93
Cuore 94
Dreams...95
Sogni..96
Be Staid 97
Remember When 98
Lifeline 101
Memories...103
Prairie 107

Cibo

Col vento nuvole passan via-
Splende il sol
E bel il suon del rosignol

Testa abassata
Sopra libro aperto
Parole esaminate ardentemente

Programmate
Digerite
Cibo per la mente
d'assorbere adesso
E quando necessarie,
Richiamare.

Cibo . . .

Food

With the wind clouds disappear
Shines the sun
And beautiful the song of the robin

Head lower'd
Above open book
Words eagerly examined

Computerized
Digested
Food for the mind
To absorb now
And when needed, recalled.

Food . . .

A. GREBAZ

Home

Night surrounds
Engulfs
While mountains reach in
And hand can almost touch
Yet remote the world
Far away it seems
Left behind
As voyager's journey home begins

Long the distance
As hours slowly fly

Weary body cries
Silent lament
To stretch, move, run . . .

Yet seated remains
While the mind
The miles devours
And distant home exited reaches,
As open arms awaiting
Eager joy display
And familiar voices fill
Long silent ears
Pouring forth words
Which gladden and overflow.

Home is the heart
      Where love is . . .

Stirred the soul
By such sight....
Yet why forgotten—
In city life?

A. GREBAZ

Nel Blu

Scia d'un aereo
Nuvola nel ciel
Lascia
E giu` il Mar del Nord
Con i suoi isolotti di ferro
  —I pozzi di petrolio—
sembran pezzi di legno
   Su un telo blu . . .
Il sole dietro la sciena
E l'ombra dell'aereo
Spicca sulle nuvole
Che circondan . . . .
   Soli nell' azzuro . . . .

In The Sky

Vapour trail of airplane
Cloud in the sky
Leaves
And below the North Sea
With its small islands of steel
      —The oil wells—
Seem pieces of wood
      Upon a canvas of blue . . .
Sun behind one's back
And the plane's shadow
Cast upon the clouds
Which surround
      Alone in the blue . . .

A. Grebaz

Alpine Landscape . . .

The water's roar
    The silence breaks
        And wind the crest sweeps—

While clouds a shroud cast
    Upon the land.

Slower the pace
    And pain to chest sends
        Message to numbed mind
           To slow down and rest.

Beauty surrounds
    As awed mind
        Unused to heights
Daily vision of mountains
    Whose tops into height
        Extend
           While waters cold and clear

Rush to valleys far bellow,
    Sparkling jewels tumbling,
        Rolling,speeding
    At breakneck pace. (con't)

A. GREBAZ

(con't)
Tree line left far behind
      As pace slows yet
            Mind goal seeks to reach . . . .

A world to see and enjoy
      Yet at same time,
            Cautious . . . .

Endeavour to, by beauty, become drunk
      On unspoiled landscape
         And savour for time
When daily pressures
      Released need be . . . .
         Memories from abysmal depths
            Recalled once more
               To enjoyed and cherished be.

Seasons

Seasons come and go
    And leaves do fall
        As trees stand still
            Without a change—
                So it seems . . .

Light and shadow—
    Entirely unnoticed
        The year's swift motion . . .

Winter's flakes fall
    Spring's rushing call
        To survey the world again
            Leaving behind freezing pain.

Summer's head high
    With a clear blue sky—
        Rushing torrents slow down
           And white waters brown
                Slowly go on by . . . .

Cheered the soul
    By life's swift flow
        And even though the world
        At end seems
        Time's wounds will slowly heal
    While seasons their silent words speak
        For us to behold and cheer
           When near's the tear . . . .

Change

Change

So difficult

Since old habits hard

To break

And binding chains,

Fears and daily lives

Upset . . .

Yet learn we

To shift and survive

Step by step . . . for . . .

Leads He (She) . . .

Through dark and dim—

Gloom splits

And on sunlit days

Ponderous weight overthrown

And life do live.

A. GREBAZ

Needs

In the silence,

In the rain,

Through the song,

Through the pain,

Where is the time

To listen to the cry,

Or wonder why

The fear and the strain ?

Hunger for food,

And need to brood,

Or hand to hold

When all around the cold,

Or mere presence there (con't)

(con't)

For someone who will care.

How filled with everyday living

That sensitivity its strength and quality

Its message hidden further 'till

The ripple of a brook,	The mere extent of hand
The reading of a book,	Seems so far . . . in distant land.—
The wind's whisper through the tree,	A stair way for the mind —
Desire to be fully free,	To seek,to reach,to find.

A. GREBAZ

Tanka (Japanese Poetry)

Snow falls down silent
While blanket ground covers
Silent the city's storm
People begin to move—
Fresh footsteps in snow appear . . . .
                    Snowstorm . . . .

Mystery Quest

Mystery
>To unravel
>>Solution seeker

The mind weaves
>Questions
>>And answer wants

Yet
>What awaits
>>When answer's finally found?

Puzzle's pieces bound
>Unforetold future
>>Holds

For seeker
>As much fun
>>To quest find

As search for the mind.

A. GREBAZ

Desert

Waste land lies
      Burning, hot,
Stifling winds
      Cracks leave
In harsh land . . .

      Sandstorms we do see
           Mirages through . . .
      Water
           Where none really is
      As ships on desert sands
         Wind.

In far sand dune
      Camel walks,
Its unseeming gait
      Ship of the desert
Wealth to wanderers
      And survival's means.

      All these and more
         The desert holds
      Along with secrets
         Buried lie.
      What tales stones could tell
           Of past and present well.

Piccole Parole

Piccole parole
      tanta importanza han
anche se semplici sembran
      cambian cio' ch'era
e da un'inverno—primavera.
      Vita sola riempion
            Con un semplice sí
      E due uniti sempre
            nel dolor e nell'amor . . . .

A. GREBAZ

Small Words

Small words
  Such importance have
Even though simple seem
  Change that which was
And from winter—spring.
  Lonely life fill
With a simple yes
  And two unite always
In pain and in love . . . .

Take Time (To . . .)

How oft
      gone
      The chance
To lift someone's
      Spirits
To simply smile
To walk in the woods
      And see . . .
To run on a sandy beach
      And see the second set
      Of footprints . . .
To wish at night
      Upon a "shooting" star
To wish the best
      For someone else . . .
All these and more
      But most of all
To say to that special someone:
      "I LOVE YOU"
So as time flies,
      do it now!!!

A. GREBAZ

Longing

Months have come
       And gone
              Yet memory

Lingers on
       As does a picture
              Of you

And name
       To mind brings
              Heart

To sing
       Wishing
              Hoping
                     Longing
                     Just merely to see you.

Ma Qualche Volta I Sogni . . .

Realta' davanti sempre c'e'
il giorno in notte
ed il tempo se ne va
in fretta assai,
mentre una volta
sensazione che non passasse mai

Cose che cambiar si posson
con altre vengon
e la realta'faccia fa'
Ma qualche volta i sogni—
di poter cambiar,
e sofferenza dissipar;
di scacciar le nuvole
quando troppa pioggia c'e'
e farle ritornar un'altro di'

Sogni a volta forza dan
d'andar avanti,
man in man,
ed anche se pene ci son
d'accettar ed il miglior far
viver il meglio che si puo' . . . .

A. GREBAZ

But Sometime The Dreams . . .

Reality in front always is
Day into night
And time goes on by . . .
Far too fast,
While once
Sensation that it would never pass.

Things that changed can be
With others come
And reality its face shows
But sometime the dreams . . . .
To be able to change,
And suffering dissipate;
To scatter the clouds
When too much rain there is
And make them come another day.

Dreams at times strength give
To continue forward,
Hand in hand,
And even if pains there are
To accept and the best to do
To live to the utmost . . .

Tree

Tree unmoving
There you lie . . . .
Your worth gone?

What of budding branch
Which sprouts from your side
And the leaves which begin
To flutter in the breeze?

Or the rain which beats
And bark decays;
But through the seasons
Are you really dead?

The soil around you grows,
And life in small seed
Quickens and flows
Itself, unknowingly, to die.

What worth then all
If unnoticed the hidden—
Or unheard the song the breeze sings
And the birds whose nest
Within you shade their home make?

A. GREBAZ

Life's capricious current
  Ebbs and flows
    Today this way
      Tomorrow who knows.

Meandering first in mischief
  Darkened dusty hill
    Then into eye-searing sunlight
      Again to move on still,

Through moss-encrusted forest
  And rocky promontory sways
    Gray slabs and tree trunks
      Of wondrous filled days

When tears as rain drop
  And oft desired but coming not
    As friendships around the bend
      By winter's bitter wind wrought

Or a single word murmured,
  Misunderstood and purpose alter
    New goals to reassess
      To strive once more and not falter

Fiery Phoenix

Fiery fierce flung clear sky
With rays as arrows
Into darkening skies speed
And mind's eye captures
For future references the sight.

Fiery Phoenix torn.
By sun's radiance
As flaming force
And world to rest begins.
People from day's worries
Slowly divest their cares
Regaining strength to face
Another new tomorrow
With its happiness or sorrow.

A. GREBAZ

Winter clouds remind
Memory swiftly
Unseen clear skies—
Hiding—
Yet soon to clear again.

Standing tall on hillside—
Patient and still,
Awaiting,
Branches cut and limbs only
Protrude naked and bare
Soon to have Man crucified
There . . . .

A. Grebaz

Geese in formation
Leader in front
Others in a 'V'
Honking as they go
To second home far below . . . .

"Somewhere The Hurt . . ."

Mile upon weary mile
Body slowly moves
The mind questing
Thoughts not thought before
And days away wore . . .

With a hop-shuffle move
The exhausting task on—
Attempt a challenge for all
One road to travel and be one;
The hurt and pain a mask
To hide behind and cheer
The task accepted gladly
Not only for self but others.

Along the journey found
Countless ways renew
A people's emotion bound
To try in own way anew.

The dream across continent took
Message by deed done
Yet even though gone
For each to take on task
And demand for us to ask
Not what others can do
But that which is for us
To do for others

For "Somewhere the hurting must stop"

Terry Fox

A. GREBAZ

Spring . . .

When new season brings—

Green

And budding trees—

Rushing waters to the seas

But most of all—

The gift to be free

From winter's freezing spell . . .

Storm . . .

Force of nature

Its voice wants heard;

Daring, challenging, crashing

Warning . . . .

The ship upon the sea,
      Its crew about tossed
by wave upon wave
      As if a cork—
Endlessly up high
      And then as fast
Swells below past . . . .

      Struggle do they
          And final hour of storm
    Clears in radiant morn
          Then steers a course for home—
    Another battle won . . . .

Wave

Wave, its source far from shore,
Speeds on its way
To crash and pound,
Or simply slide gently
Upon deserted or crowded beach
For eager one to reach
And upon to bravely surf.
Wades the form far out
And distance decided reached
Stands upon slim board
As with a curdling shout
Challenge begins—
To beat the wave
Or beaten be.
Challenge to body and mind
To strive and accomplish
Deed not done before;
To reach beyond the everyday
And ride dangerously high
As on a bucking horse
But even worse—
The thunder of nature.
Force uplifts into the air
As daunting surfer will dare
Hoping to survive
And once more onward move—
Again one's courage to prove . . .

A. GREBAZ

Le Tre Cime Del Lavaredo

Le tue cime nuvolose
tant 'alte e favolose
che tanta gente vien
per veder vista ben.

Da distanze non imaginabile
attraverso mari e terre lontane
per veder le tue vette
ed in distanza Misurina
poi scriver,una rima
passando il tempo estivo
quando l'inverno fa privo.

Veloce il pensiero
transporta sul sentiero
dove, nomi con sasso scritti
sull' erba e strada fitti

Tempo presto e ' passato cosi'
Da voler esser ancora li'
Dove I 'inverno tutto bianco copre
e I 'estate verdastro apre.

Piede pesante calpesta
Insu oppure ingiú
A valle o a vetta
desiderio tale meta
che vita ogni via
possa sulle vette altro dia'.

The Three Peaks Of The Lavaredo

Your cloudy peaks
So high and famous
That many people come
To see the sight well.

From distance unimaginable
Across seas and from distant lands
To see your peaks
And in the distance, Misurina
To write a rhyme
Passing the summer holidays
When winter's far away.

Fast is the thought
That carries to the path
Where names where written with stones
On the grass and at road's side.

Time has flown by so fast
That the wish's to be there again
Where winter covers all in white
And summer everything green makes.

A heavy foot does thread
While the head's raised high
Returning always quickly
Up there or down
To valley or peak
Desire such goal
That life's every road
May pass amongst the peaks another day.

A. Grebaz

*The Lavaredo—a group of mountain peaks Northeast of Cortina, Italy

*Misurina—small village at the bottom of the mountain

Sleeping Village

Early morn upon the land
When village asleep lies,
    And snowy blanket covers,
    Then silence reigns best.
    But all this broken
When church bells knell
    And peal with loud ring—
    Its sound surrounding bring
    With such speed alight
Upon mountain sides might,
    Not recognizing danger
    Which steep heights touches
    And slow at first, then faster,
Wall of white moves

    Down at breaking speed racing
    As rumble all else pacing . . . .

Village's tower only stands
    Unburried but tattered
    By such force battered
    As sleepy souls rest
Some to wake no more
    Others reaching for a door
    By which from tomb escape (con't)

A. GREBAZ

(con't)
Resourcefulness arms move at will
    To empty the void filled,
    To find much needed air,
While sweat down cold foreheads spreads . . . .
    Concerned news outer world
    Do finally reach
    As rescue's on the way
But for many too late the work
    As sun's rays beyond the hill
    Do send their faint warmth.

Torches light dark night
    To bring new hope alight
    And sobbing eyes look
    For familiar faces 'till

Here a greeting, there a cry
And news from wall to wall rings.

New day the labour sees
    Yet entire village not free
    From icy cold grip—
Wrenched by determined will
    But slow the progress still.

    Melting snow to water turns
When spring's sun does burn
    And clenching, clutching fist
    Of avalanche's faceless form
Releases once more

    But decision to be made
    To remain else goodbye to bade
Or lifetime's work begins to fade,
    Anew the will to strive and survive . . . .

Una Rosa Tra Le Spine (Tina)

Il seme e' caduto all 'insaputo,
Sienzioso dal vento portato,

Occupo' cosi' un po'
D' arrida terra.

Tra le spine germoglio'
Faccendosi un posto
In quell angolo-una vita.
Al passante l'occhio tiro'
Quando i petali s' appriron
Ed al mondo mostro'
La belleza e bonta'
Che fin quell di'
All 'insaputa cresceva
Con scopo la vita insaputo
Ma il vuoto riempí
E per ciascuno era lí—
Una rosa nel giardino . . . .

Ora ch'e l'inverno, non piu 'vicina,
Ma forza a memoria
E calor nel cuor
Da viver ed amar—
Vita per il momento
Ma quando vissuta
Ne vale cento . . . .

A. GREBAZ

A Rose Among The Thorns (Tina)

The seed fallen who knows when,
Silently carried by the wind,

Took up such a small amount
Of dry ground.

Among the thorns it grew
Making its place
In that corner—a life
The passer's—by eye did catch
When the petals open'd
And to the world showed
The beauty and goodness
That until that day
Unknown it grew
With purpose in life who knew
But the emptiness filled
And for everyone was there—
A rose in the garden . . . .

Now that it's winter, no more here,
But strength in the memory
And warmth in the heart
To live and to love—
Life for the moment
But when lived
Worth a hundred . . . .

A. GREBAZ

Midnight Solitudes . . .

From deep within
Desires drive
Burning flesh
To feverish heights
Yet mind struggles to quench
Threatening thirst
And pulsing blood
Does slowly settle
To normal once again
      But still left
          The pain . . .

———————————

Horse in Forest
      Lost
      Astray runs the wind
          Where is home?
(Home seeks its way)

———————————

Swans in pond
Ripples send
To distant shore
      Motion

Solitudini Notturne . . .

Dal profondo interno
Desiderii sforzano
La pelle rovente
Ad altezze fevrili
Ma la mente cerca di smorzare
La sete minacciante
Ed il sangue palpitante
Si calma poco a poco
Al normale un altra volta
    Ma cio' che rimane
        Il dolore . . .

———————

Cavallo nella foresta
    Perso
    Il vento soffia e via
        Dov'e il casale?
(La casa richlama)

———————

Cigni al lagheto
Onde mandano
Alla sponda distante
    Movimento

Faces

Faces in a crowd
Own aura cast
And personality
Behind a mask hidden
But into immediate space
Do ripples' send
And encroachers feud
Afraid to reach
For out stretched hand seeking
Misunderstood or deeply rooted.
    Society's changing mood
    A mess has made
    And strangers we—
    Worried more of self
    Than of fading cries
    Roaring waves do in uproar—
        Quell . . .

Face

Face in una folla
Ogn'una la sua aura
E personalita'
Dietro una maschera nascoste
Ma nello spazio vicino
Mandano onde
E oltrepassanti lottano
Paurosi di prendere
La mano estesa che cerca
Sottintesi o piantati profondamente
    Il pensato della gente cambia
    Ed un pasticcio ha creato
    Ed estranei noi—
    Pensando piú a noi stessi
    Che ai gridi che spariscono
    Le onde sonore e rumorose
      Soffocano . . .

     A. GREBAZ

Life

While crowd passed by
Hurrying, scurrying who knows where
Spur of the moment moves
Or just by chance
Meeting strangers
Alone no more—
A smile, a shy "hello"
And open closed door
If will but wants—
Society's walls tumbling—
No more alone.

    Seldom before taken
    Outstretched hand
    In such a way
    For heart to speak
    And meaning understood
    The need for company
    But more

Companion soul to speak seek
Long journey but a step
Yet footfall side by side
Seeking mutual goal

    To share and live
    Life . . .

Vita

Mentre la folla passa vicino
In fretta e furia chi sa dove
All imprevisto muove
Oppure per caso
Incontrando sconosciuti
Soli non piú—
Un sorriso, un semplice "Ciao"
E la porta chiusa s'apre
Se si vuole
Le mura sociali cadono
Non piú soli.

  Poche volte presa prima
  La mano stesa
  In tal modo
  Per cuori da parlarsi
  E le parole capite
  La necessita di compagnia
  Ma di piú

Lo spirito compagno a cui parlare chiedere
Viaggio lungo ma un piede
Mentre piede a piede
Cercando le stesse mete

  Da dare l'uno a l'atra e vivere
  Vita . . .

A. Grebaz

Rocks above
Kakabeka Falls
Provincial Park (ON)

A. GREBAZ

Life's Meaning . . .

Life's meaning
Hidden still
Behind half-open doorway
Glimmer in the distance
 Yet unknown
 Its message as a puzzle
 To put in place.
  Day by day
  New surprises-sad or gay
  Controlled at times
   Yet, at times,
    Beyond one's power.

Sleeping, walking, waking
 Monotony broken
 By one's own desire
 Deed to create for each
  An earthly heaven
   Or a living hell

Until the time to say
 Farewell
 Step by step
 The child to man grows
  And slowly or suddenly
   Learns life's meaning.

A. GREBAZ

Summer its golden head
     Rises
Above silver-gray cloud
     And casts its heated rays
To awaiting earth below.

     Green the grass,
Gold the grain,
     Dispelled the cold—
For a spell at least.

     Glowing and full of life,
World awakes eager
     The chance to take
And enjoy fully
     Summer's enchanting spell

Gathering the joy—
     Harvest stored
To long winter last.

The Ball

Slow at start
        Then faster and faster
As a rushing torrent
        The beat picks up.

Swaying to the sound
        Keeping time—The beat pleasant—
        The crowd willing

Time goes on by—

        Little lady, don't be shy—
And let the feet move—
        Company to hold;
Even though for a while.

        The early hours come. . . .
The slipper fallen,
        Lost along the way;
Fair prince searches
        And hopefully finds,
Another day . . . .
        Cinderella . . . .

A. GREBAZ

Where Eagles Fly . . .

In clear blue sky
Where no one else's around
A speck in open space
Far from the rushing race
Where mountains to sky bound
There to let out a joyful cry.

From rushing rivers steep
And forests clinging deep
Or calm mirrored lake
Mountain's feet do rake
Trails few left behind
And new trail in the mind
To walk where few have done
'Till the day's sun is gone
And at shadows fall
To hear the eerie call
Of far—reaching loon
A day worth living—boon.

Footprints soon gone
From rocky mountain terrain
And deep snows chilling bone
Upon one's own reliance main;
Nature's storehouse on to gaze
Removing world's rushing haze
Recharging body's cells more
Troubled self once again restore.

_____

Spider your web spins
Strong winds to withstand
Sparkling jewel in the sun.

La Scogliera Dei Sogni Perduti

Spiaggia brucciante sabbiosa
dove gente viene a divertirsi
sole cocente ed acque
                    turbolenti
scogli massivi trappola fan
per nave buttate come foglie
dondolanti su un mare pazzo
verso riva mordente van
morenti i sogni di vita
sulla scogliera dei sogni perduti . . . .
Tormenta vincitrice ancor . . .

———————————

Ragno la tua rete stendi
Da sopravivere i venti forti—
Gioiello che splende al sole.

The Cliff Of Lost Dreams . . .

Burning sandy shore
Where people come to enjoy themselves
Burning sun and turbulent waters

Massive cliffs trap do make
For ships thrown like leaves
Bobbing up and down on a crazy sea
Towards the deadly shore
Dying dreams of life
On the cliff of lost dreams . . .
Storm winner once more . . .

Storms . . .

Tossing, turning cauldron
    Boils
Fearful sight to behold
    Much more
To partaker be.
        Wave upon wave the shore
            Pounds
            Wearing down ages' work,
                Reshaping.
Such can be life
    But then
Shines the sun upon the sea

    Calm the waters
As new day dawns—
    A future to shape
And hope to carry on reinforced—
        A challenge to conquer
New mountains to climb
        New seas to sail . . .

A. GREBAZ

Foresta Boreale . . .

Sperduto nella foresta estesa
dov 'acqua piu' che terra c 'e'
e moltitudini i colli
sperduti all' orizonte.
fitta foresta ombrosa
dove il sole un lumicino sembra
Paurosamente il perdersi
possibilita'

e perder direzione con tan'facilitá.

Terra del Shield Canadese
Paesaggio selvaggio
tanta bellezza ha
d'attirar indietro
ogni volta che lasciar
Si va.

Solitudine maestosa
di pace e silenzio
dove poca gente c 'e'
sperduta nei paeselli
uniti solamente
dalla strada maestra
che attraversa
ed il viaggiante via
se ne va. (con't)

(con't)
Segno di vita qua e lá
Ma natura selvaggia
con mano sua doma
e ristringe al seno.

Rimane solamente
Il coraggio
Che natura combatter sa.

Terra Meastosa
al piede del Lago Superiore
estesa nell' infinitá.

Canadian Shield . . .

Lost in the endless forest
    Where there is more water than land,
And countless hills
Lost in the horizon
Thick shadowy forest
Where the sun appears to be a small candle
Fearful! possibility—getting lost

And losing direction so easily.

Land of the Canadian Shield—
Savage land
So beautiful is
To attract back again
Each time one leaves it.

Majestic solitude
Of peace and silence
Where few people live—
Lost in small villages
United only
By the ribbon of highway
That crosses it
And the traveler
Goes away again. (con't)

(con't)
Sign of life here and there
But savage nature
With her hand rules
And takes back to her breast

There remains only
The courage
Which knows how to fight
Nature.

Majestic land
At the foot of Lake Superior
Spread out into infinity.

Quench, Oh Pen

Stilled for so long,
     run with the wind
and let the dreams fill
     the void and begin,
again,
     your work,oh pen.

Speak the words which deep
within the inner depths
     Dwell.

Crash upon the outer wall
     as waves upon the shore
          resounding distance away.

Strengthen the desire
     and let the heights
          Reach,
the empty voids fill,
and words, flow
     as a river
          Rushing to the sea.

Forget the silences behind
     but look ahead
          To each new challenge—
     Each new goal around
to fill and inner burning—
     QUENCH!!!

A. GREBAZ

Sazia, O Penna

Silenziosa per tanto tempo,
Corri col vento
E lascia che i sogni riempiano
Il vuoto ed incomincia,
Di nuovo,
il tuo lavoro, o penna.

Parla le parole che profonde
Negli abissi interni
Vivono.

Sbatti contro le mura esterne
come onde contro la sponda
Che si sentono in distanza.

Rinforza il desiderio
E le cime
Raggiungi,
I vuoti riempi
E parole, fai scorrere
Come un fiume
Che in fretta va al mare.

Dimentica i silenzi passati
Ma guarda avanti
Ad ogni nuova meta—
Ogni nuova sfida da sorpassare
Da riempire ed il fuoco interno
SODISFA!!!

A rose among the thorns . . .
　　Does its way weave
towards sunlight
　　Where its beauty
displayed in splendor
　　Remains.

　　Behold the beauty
and heart fills
　　With new fragrance
for among life's path
　　Strange,unexpected meetings
and new friendships made
　　Some for a while
others for a lifetime.

A. GREBAZ

Una rosa tra le spine
Si fa strada
Verso la luce del sole
Dove la sua belezza
Esposta con splendore
Rimane.

Guarda la belezza
Che il cuore riempie
Col nuovo profumo
Dal sentiero della vita
Incontri strani ed inaspettati
E nuove amicizie si fanno
Alcune per un po'
Altre per tutta la vita.

Clouds
	But pass on by—
		Blown away

By the radiance
	Of your smile
		Or encouraging word

You have for those around you
		Letting not a frown
				But a cheer
Be your companion.

Nuvole
      Ma se ne vanno
            Soffiate via

Dal splendore
      Del tuo sorriso
            O da una parola sollevante

Che tu hai per quelli vicino a te
      Non lasciando una cattiveria
            Ma un incoraggiamento
Essere il tuo amico (compagno).

You . . .

A door opened—
       Unseen—
And you became
       A part of me;
For where're I go
       There you are
For soul's opened
       And mere glance
Will do.

       To hurt not part—
           Wishing the best for you . . .

A. GREBAZ

Once Upon A Seashore

Sand the waves wore
    Grains,
        Powder,
            From ponderous granites—
       Continuous pounding motion—
        Destiny.

Youth sand castles did build
     Yet waves in time—
        The shore did claim—
          Again.

Wise man a dream followed—
     The ocean wishing to cross
        Set his mark—
          A dock, a wharf—

Steel and concrete fought
     Relentless sea . . .
        Yet, with time . . . .
            Returns the shore . . .

Each Day . . .

It's the living
    that's harder—
Each day a new
    decision along the way—

A challenge or retreat,
    a victory or defeat,
in which each has
    a say
a yes or no—
    taking us much further,
along roads to follow
    or avoid . . .

A. GREBAZ

Ogni Giorno . . .

E' il viver
        ch 'e ' il piú difficile
ogni giorno una nuova
        decisione per via—

Una sfida o una ritirata,
        una vittoria o un disfatta,
In cui ogn 'uno c 'ha
        Un dire
Un si ' o un no—
        portandoci piu' lontano,
Per vie da seguire
        o evitare . . .

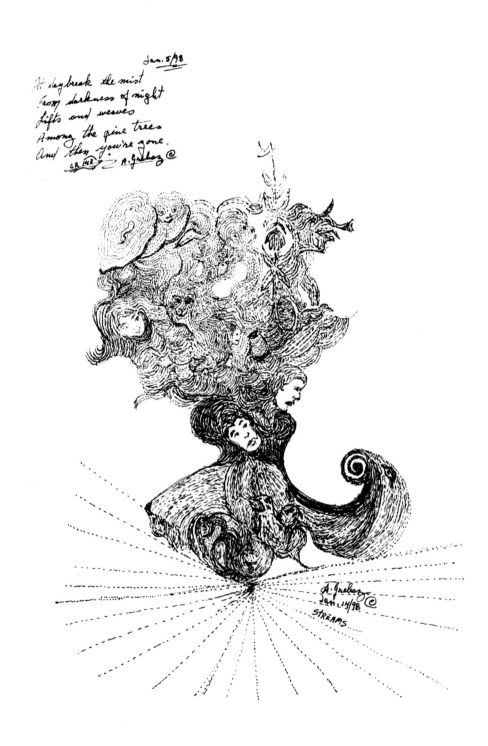

At daybreak the mist
From darkness of night
Lifts and weaves
Among the pine trees
And then you're gone.
— A. Grebaz

A. GREBAZ

Creativity

burning

yearning

Fiery desire

    To create

    To shape

        What inner soul feels,

        Sees, desires, expects,

        Wishes, wants,

Not only for self

But for others

To share with,

        To enjoy,

        Or portray

    That which one would like

The world around

To be —

A place of harmony

Sliver Of A Moon

Low upon horizon

Peeks its form

And clouds

Thrust on by

Sliver of a moon

Skies still dark

City still asleep

Sounds carrying

Yet in stillness

Beauty

A. GREBAZ

In silence peace.

Footsteps with their crunch

Thrill

And air sharp
            Stinging,
                    Invigorating
            The cobwebs removes

        And thoughts fly
From dormant depth

New day new challenge
        New dreams,
Desires,
        Striving
Not to merely do
        But self to higher peaks
Climb and reach

A Walk In Time

A walk in snow—covered field,

    If you will;

Nothing there but snow—

    Someone will say . . .

Yet look again,

    A blade of grass here,

      A hand—full of seed

        Wind-blown there;

          And again—footprints—

        Like strange twigs—

      Of birds—everywhere.

    A print in snow (con't)

A. GREBAZ

(con't)
Its story tells

Look again—well—

The stem of a wild flower,

Its leaves preserved—

By wintry ice—

Attracts the eye

And mind begins

Its wondering—

Beauty still abounds . . .

Harbingers Of Spring

Cloudy skies
    Their warning bring
Of storm's approach—
    Trees majestically sway
This wet wintry day.

    Fearful force fascinates
Its fury unleashed—
    Waves upon icy surface
Havoc create—awash the shore
    With squall's stinging bite
And snow melts and runs off
    Fear of flood a dread.

    Yet through all this
    Harbingers of spring
Their eerie cries fling
    As bodies up-swung
Unseen currents of air uplift—
    Fearless in storm's face
Flight continued on
    From sea far away
Once more they've come to stay
    'Till fierce November storms
Will force them on their way.

Seagulls fling their cry
    Upon wind's wings
To uplift slumbering land
    From its winter spell.

    Uplift, oh soul
    For spring's on its way
    And cheerful song sings today.

A. GREBAZ

A Heart Of Stone

Hard granite in the sunshine
Heated but at surface
While in the depths cold
    Hand outstretched, unseen,
    Nor cry for help heard.

When into icy abyss
We fall —
To whom do we call
If not each other?
    Of what value then
    If our backs we turn
Because of fear
And let the cries for help
    Unheeded be?

In all the turmoil and haste
So much energy we waste
Yet amidst the noise and dim
We can always rely upon —
    Him—
    Whose life for us gave,
    For us to live beyond the grave.

Then turn, o heart of stone,
Into a heart of flesh,
Following in His footsteps
'Though rocky and hard may
    Be the way
    Living as He did
    To the best, every day.

L. superior - Islands ...

A. GREBAZ

Mare . . .

Mentre il gabbiano
      Sulle onde balla
Il vento il suo grido
      Mi porta,
ed il mare col suo mistero
      Attira.

Ipnotico il richiamo
      Ed il conoscer il desir
ma all'orizonte il temporale
E turbolenti le onde rapaci . . .
Salvezza alla sponda

Sea . . .

While the seagull
       Dances on the waves—
The wind its cry
       Carries to me,
And the sea with its mystery
       Attracts.

Hypnotic its call
       And to know the desire
But on the horizon the storm
       And the hungry waves toss . . . .
Safety on shore.

A. Grebaz

Someday . . .

Places seen,

People meet,

Time to return

To times gone by . . .

Revisit . . .

Thoughts and desires fulfilled . . . .

The reality

Its clutches

Extends

And all that's left . . . .

Someday . . .

Forse Un Giorno . . .

Posti visti
Gente incontrata,
E' ora di ritornare
    Ai tempi passati . . .

Rivisitare . . .

    Pensieri e desiderii sodisfatti . . .
Poi la realta'
    I suoi artigli
        Estende
        E tutto cio' che rimane . . .
    Un giorno forse . . .

A. GREBAZ

Angel eyes
        Seen
                In close depths
Of crowded throng
        Slowly swing
                Studying
                        Sizing
                        Encompassing
                                Enthralling
With their magnetic touch.

Longing for comfort
        Of human touch
                Of gentle hand
                        To rest upon
                        Arm extended
                Yet just as sudden
        Vision disappears
And crowd
Surging dizzily by—
Hides.

Forgotten not
        Need much stronger
For human touch
        To enfold
                And thus comfort
                From uncaring throng
And wounds to heal . . .

Words, Like A Fountain Flow . . .

Beauty's delight

Beam of radiant sunlight
Upon golden crest
Falls

Sunrise its beauty
Astounds
Hues swirl
Starry sky fading.

New dawn
Stream fills
With resplendent diamonds
Twinkling,
Sparkling,
Dazzling,

Eye's delight
Surpassed by inner feeling

Beauty's delight
Distant forms
Gray hued—white crests
Majestically rise
From slumber's spell
Wave upon wave
As sun rising form

Silenzio

Il silenzio delle montagne
Lo spirit desidera
Perché
Il mondo—
Pieno di distrazioni
E'.
L'aria fresca
Viene a risvegliare
E la mente
Piu' lavora
Ed inspirata e'.

La neve-un manto bianco—
Distesa
Sulle piste

Ed I strapiombi
Che desiderian esser
Conquistati

Piede vuol camminar
Su cime senza nome
E ripidi gole vertiginose
A passar.

Aquila-il tuo volo
Nell' azzur
Trabbagliante—
Magiestoso . . .

Tutto l'occhio interno
In un istante
Vede
Ed il cuore
Desidera . . . .

Intensamente.

A. GREBAZ

Silence

Silence of mountains
Spirit desires
For
The world
Full of distractions—
Is.
The fresh air
Comes to awaken
And the mind
Works more
And inspired is—

Snow—a white mantle
Spread out
On the ski trails
And the abysses
Want to be
Conquered.

Foot wishes to walk
On peaks without name
And steep vertiginous gorges
To pass.

A. GREBAZ

Eagle—your flight
In the blue sky—
Blinding—
Majestic . . . .

All the interior eye
In an instant
Sees
And the heart
Desires . . .

Intensly.

A. GREBAZ

Heart

Heart,
        Why such a beat?
Exited?
        Frustrated?
Trusted someone
        Too much?

Or is it the everyday
        Struggle
of living
        Oppressed by self
or by others . . .

        What then
Of friends,
        or relatives,
or stranger's words,
        to help slow down
or rise again?
        And look upon
each tomorrow
        As a better day.

Cuore . . .

Cuore,
       come mai questo battito?
Eccitato?
      Dilluso?
Ti sei fidato di qual'cuno
      Troppo?

O e' la lotta
      d'ogni di'
di vivere·
      oppresso da te stesso
o dagli altri . . .

    Che allora
degli amici,
      parenti,
di parole d'un estraneo,
      di rallentarti
o aiutarti ad alzare?
      Guarda
ogni domani
      come un giomo migliore.

A. GREBAZ

Dreams

Fiery dragons and pressures
And things-
Of such—dreams—
Yet what life,
If dreams not
Dreamer?

Challenges
Whence for
To strive
or conquer
or binding chains
To break—
If not from inner self?

Sogni

Draghi in fiamme o oppressioni
E cose-
Tali —sogni—
Ma che vita,
Se non sogna
Il sognatore?

Sfide
Allora perche
Lottare,
o conquistare
O le catene che
Incatenano—spezzare?
Se no per la persona in noi?

A. GREBAZ

Be Staid

Be staid
        For once, o wondrous heart,
Not play for others' wish a part
        But self upright stand
Whether at home or in foreign land
        The wisdom of nature's ways
        The voice from inner heart plays
        The cruelties of war-at worst abhor . . . .
        The turbulence let not overcome, for shore,
        Hill, and men, in time all pass for sure . . . .
                Yet through it all,
                But not afraid.

Remember When

Remember when
    Streets were an ice rink
        As wintry storm did descend
            Upon quiet, sleeping city
            Without a single moment of pity.

        Children full of glee
    Skating on icy sheet
From momentary cares free . . . .

    Hard press'd drivers beware
        For sudden burst of speed
          Is all one really needs
        To spin as a top turns
      And afterwards awareness burns
    While full well remembered
Nature's furious force tempered . . .

A. GREBAZ

A. Grebaz
Dec. 20/99

Life's capricious current
    ebbs and flows—
        Today this way
            Tomorrow who knows.
Meandering first in mischief
    Darkened dusty hill
        Then into eye-searing sunlight
            Again to move on still,
Through moss-encrusted forest
    And rocky promontory sway
        Gray slabs and tree trunks
            Of wondrous filled days
When tears as rain drop
    And oft desired but coming not
        As friendships around the bend
            By winter's bitter wind wrought
Or a single word murmured—
    Misunderstood and purpose alter
        New goals to reassess
            To strive once more and not falter

A. GREBAZ

Lifeline

From tower's underside

    Strung out to hang and dry,

Long ribbons-white once more—

    Are readied to spring to life

        At hand's instant pressure.

What journey you have made

    From stores to red forest flames

    And back again.

You have seen men sweat

    In face of fiery flash

And billowing clouds of smoke

    Choking, acrid, pungent-smell

Of burning forest's flesh

    While water, from once

        Clear lakes and rushing torrents,

Now mere trickle by Summer's heat,

    Compressors hastily pump

Through your long slender form

    To push back and keep

Nature's long hard work

    From becoming mere charred land. (con't)

A. GREBAZ

(con't)

Long hours of work

     Day after weary day,

Muscles and minds wear down

     As constant battle fought

To still the flinging flames

     And beauty's life upkeep

In harsh Northland

     Of forest, lakes, and rocks

          Canadian Shield . . . .

     Storehouse of unbounded wealth

Guardians (try) to maintain

     While nature's claim furiously

Clutches and won't let go.

     At long last, well deserved rest

Ready for another day's test.

     'till Summer's scorching heat be over

And Fall's humid, restoring rains

     Return forest to its beauty again.

A. GREBAZ

Memories

How is it
    That wherever we go-
        A little rock here—
            An oak seed there—
                A postcard from everywhere—
                We take along with us?
                Is it to sing a sweet song
            When wintery winds blow
        The streets full of snow
    Or to remind us of
When gray the skies above.
Of those times we had
That was not so sad?
    When life seems so bad
        We look at what we had
            And a smile to replace
                A tear
                    And a smile to replace
                        Inner fear
                        And even 'though
                    Dear ones gone
                They return with us
        And we're not alone.

Sand sifts
    Restless
        Through the Eons
           Non-stop—
              Drifting
                  Through space and time
                 Wind
                      Its friend
                         Blowing fierce
                    Or slow
                Yet ever moving
              With such meticulous care
          Working
        To become eventually
                  Infinity . . .

A. GREBAZ

Gently the hair's brushed

From deeply pensive forehead

As the brush strokes,

Measured and certain,

Fall upon the canvas

And a work of art—

Created . . .

Cold

The weather

Ice the water

Ships at dockside . . . unmoving

Long the winter

Awaited for spring

So far away.

A. GREBAZ

Prairie

Mile upon mile
     Unbroken
Lies the land
     Monotonous
Flat
     Without a break in night
Trees few and scattered
     As if to taunt traveler
To find shade
     In heat of summer day
And warm shelter
     In cold wintry spell

Black ribbon cuts
     Across endless plain
Mesmerizing spell
     As ahead rushes traveller
to get to other side.

Here and there
     In distant diamond's flight
Comfort momentarily found—
     There are others around.

Then, once again,
     Endless mile upon endless mile
All the while
     Wondering when it will end . . .

Names long given
     Forgotten reason why
Upon roadway mark
     Man's mere effort
To tame a wild land

CPSIA information can be obtained at www.ICGtesting.com
Printed in the USA
LVOW040012021111

253064LV00002B/16/P